★ It's My State! ★ ★ ★ ★

LOUISIANA
The Pelican State

Ruth Bjorklund and Andy Steinitz

Cavendish Square
New York

Published in 2015 by Cavendish Square Publishing, LLC
243 5th Avenue, Suite 136, New York, NY 10016

Website: cavendishsq.com

This publication represents the opinions and views of the author based on his or her personal experience, knowledge, and research. The information in this book serves as a general guide only. The author and publisher have used their best efforts in preparing this book and disclaim liability rising directly or indirectly from the use and application of this book.

CPSIA Compliance Information: Batch #WS14CSQ

All websites were available and accurate when this book was sent to press.

Library of Congress Cataloging-in-Publication Data
Bjorklund, Ruth.
 Louisiana / Ruth Bjorklund, Andy Steinitz. — Third edition.
    pages cm. — (It's my state!)
 Includes index.
 ISBN 978-1-62712-740-0 (hardcover) ISBN 978-1-62712-742-4 (ebook)
 1. Louisiana—Juvenile literature. I. Steinitz, Andy. II. Title.
 F369.3.B58 2014
 976.3—dc23
                    2014006275

Editorial Director: Dean Miller
Editor, Third Edition: Nicole Sothard
Art Director: Jeffrey Talbot
Series Designer, Third Edition: Jeffrey Talbot
Layout Design, Third Edition: Erica Clendening
Production Manager: Jennifer Ryder-Talbot

Printed in the United States of America

LOUISIANA

CONTENTS

State Flower: Magnolia

Magnolia trees can be found in swamps, lowland forests, and coastal plains. Some reach a height of 100 feet (30 meters). Flowers bloom in early summer in a number of colors, from white to purple to yellow.

State Bird: Brown Pelican

Brown pelicans were once so abundant in Louisiana that its nickname is the Pelican State. But brown pelicans nearly became extinct, or died out, in the 1950s. The birds were eating a pesticide called DDT, which made their eggs break easily. DDT was banned in 1972, and conservationists have since helped restore the brown pelican population.

State Tree: Bald Cypress

The bald cypress is a conifer, a type of tree that usually keeps its needlelike leaves year-round. But the bald cypress sheds its needles in winter, which is how the tree got its name. Bald cypresses grow in warm coastal areas and swamps. They can live for several hundred years.

LOUISIANA
POPULATION: 4,533,372

★ State Mammal: Louisiana Black Bear

Louisiana black bears weigh up to 400 pounds (180 kg). They are shy creatures, making their homes in hollow logs, briar patches, and brush piles. By 1992, the population of Louisiana black bears had shrunk so low that the animals were declared threatened. Today, only around 500 bears are left. Louisianans are working to prevent their state mammal from dying out.

★ State Crustacean: Crawfish

In 1983, Louisiana became the first state to select an official state crustacean. Crawfish are small freshwater cousins to the sea-dwelling lobster. Found in marshes, rivers, lakes, ponds, and swamps throughout the state, crawfish have been a flavorful and important source of food for centuries.

★ State Dog: Catahoula Leopard Dog

The Catahoula leopard dog is a breed that probably developed in the 1500s when residents of the region bred dogs raised by Native Americans with dogs brought from Spain. The Catahoula leopard dog has shiny eyes, a spotted coat, and webbed feet that are useful for swimming. Most of these dogs are good hunters and trackers.

Brown pelicans are gray-brown birds with yellow heads. They have thin necks, and their bills have a stretchy pouch that is used for capturing fish.

The Pelican State

L ush, watery Louisiana seems forever in bloom. Billions of gallons of river water wash through the state and spill out into the Gulf of Mexico. Boundless streams, bayous (marshy creeks), lakes, ponds, swamps, and marshlands bathe the land and give life to a rich variety of vegetation and wildlife.

Louisiana is one of the most unique states in the country. Because of its rich history, Louisiana is influenced by Spanish, French, and African culture. That is evident in the food, dance, and music. Louisianans know where they live is special, and they are proud of where they come from. There is no other place like it.

Prairies to the Sea

The state of Louisiana is a boot-shaped area of land covering about 43,560 square miles (112,820 sq km). More than 8,200 square miles (21,200 sq km) are underwater. The state is divided into 64 parishes. These divisions are known as counties in most other states. The state capital, Baton Rouge, is in East Baton Rouge Parish. New Orleans, the largest city in Louisiana, is in Orleans Parish, in the southeastern part of the state.

Waves hit the Chandeleur Islands, a chain of barrier islands off the southeastern coast of Louisiana.

Louisiana Borders

North: Arkansas

South: Gulf of Mexico

East: Mississippi

West: Texas

One of the nation's most important rivers, the Mississippi River, meanders through the state. The Mississippi empties into the Gulf of Mexico, as do other rivers in Louisiana, such as the Atchafalaya, Ouachita, Sabine, Pearl, and Red rivers. Many areas of Louisiana are low-lying wetlands, swamps, and marshes. However, the state also has rolling hills, forests, and grass prairies. The highest point in the state, Driskill Mountain, is located in northwestern Louisiana and rises 535 feet (163 m). The lowest points are near the coast, where the land dips below sea level. Just off the coast, many islands protect the delicate inner shore. These islands are called barrier islands.

The Gulf Coastal Plain

The entire state of Louisiana is part of a natural geographic region called the Gulf Coastal Plain. The Tunica Hills lie in a group of parishes known as the Florida Parishes in the eastern part of the state. Covered with flowering trees such as magnolia, sweetgum, dogwood, and hydrangea, the Tunica Hills also feature forests of beech, oak, and other hardwoods. Nearby West Feliciana Parish contains the wetlands and woodlands where the great **naturalist** John Audubon studied and painted wildlife for his famous book Birds of America. While exploring the region, Audubon painted more than eighty birds, including the hooded merganser, pigeon hawk, white pelican, and blue heron, as well as the now-extinct passenger pigeon.

The Pearl River forms the state's southeastern border with Mississippi. The Pearl River splits into many channels and small, marshy, slow-moving waterways called bayous. These bayous and channels form large swamps and marshlands where trees are draped with Spanish moss. Honey Island Swamp, near Slidell, is the largest in the area. There, bald eagles, alligators, egrets, and wild turkeys roam among the oaks, cypress, and water lilies. More than 50 square miles (130 sq km) of pristine wetland is filled with wild creatures and plants.

Rainwater carved grooves into this reconstructed levee in New Orleans.

LOUISIANA
POPULATION BY PARISH

Parish	Population	Parish	Population	Parish	Population
Acadia Parish	61,773	Lafourche Parish	96,318	Vermilion Parish	57,999
Allen Parish	25,764	LaSalle Parish	14,890	Vernon Parish	52,334
Ascension Parish	107,215	Lincoln Parish	46,735	Washington Parish	47,168
Assumption Parish	23,421	Livingston Parish	128,026	Webster Parish	41,207
Avoyelles Parish	42,073	Madison Parish	12,093	West Baton Rouge Parish	23,788
Beauregard Parish	35,654	Morehouse Parish	27,979	West Carroll Parish	11,604
Bienville Parish	14,353	Natchitoches Parish	39,566	West Feliciana Parish	15,625
Bossier Parish	116,979	Orleans Parish	343,829	Winn Parish	15,313
Caddo Parish	254,969	Ouachita Parish	153,720		
Calcasieu Parish	192,768	Plaquemines Parish	23,042		
Caldwell Parish	10,132	Pointe Coupee Parish	22,802		
Cameron Parish	6,839	Rapides Parish	131,613		
Catahoula Parish	10,407	Red River Parish	9,091		
Claiborne Parish	17,195	Richland Parish	20,725		
Concordia Parish	20,822	Sabine Parish	24,233		
De Soto Parish	26,656	St. Bernard Parish	35,897		
East Baton Rouge Parish	440,171	St. Charles Parish	52,780		
East Carroll Parish	7,759	St. Helena Parish	11,203		
East Feliciana Parish	20,267	St. James Parish	22,102		
Evangeline Parish	33,984	St. John the Baptist Parish	45,924		
Franklin Parish	20,767	St. Landry Parish	83,384		
Grant Parish	22,309	St. Martin Parish	52,160		
Iberia Parish	73,240	St. Mary Parish	54,650		
Iberville Parish	33,387	St. Tammany Parish	233,740		
Jackson Parish	16,274	Tangipahoa Parish	121,097		
Jefferson Parish	432,552	Tensas Parish	5,252		
Jefferson Davis Parish	31,594	Terrebonne Parish	111,860		
Lafayette Parish	221,578	Union Parish	22,721		

Source: U.S. Bureau of the Census, 2010

Orleans Parish

East Baton Rouge Parish

A young explorer paddles a boat down the Atchafalaya River in southern Louisiana.

The Mississippi Floodplain is an area of fertile land that lies along the banks of the famous river that winds through the state. The major cities of New Orleans and Baton Rouge are found in the Floodplain. Over time, the river has reshaped the surrounding landscape. Levees, or ridges 10 to 15 feet (3 to 5 m) high, stop the river from flooding nearby areas. Some levees have formed naturally as sediment—rocks, dirt, sand, and other material—is pushed up onto land by the river as it flows or floods. People also build levees or strengthen natural levees with sediment or concrete. Beyond the levee walls, the land is very flat and filled with ponds, swamps, and bayous. Slight changes in ground level cause these areas to collect rain and floodwater.

The southern end of the Mississippi River opens into a delta. The river delta is a system of slow-moving channels of water and rich, muddy soil. There, the Mississippi drops about 500 million tons (453 million metric tons) of soil every year. When the mud blocks a channel, the water pushes through to form a new route.

The entire coast west of the delta into Texas is an estuary, where the fresh water of the Mississippi River and its offshoots meets the salty water of the Gulf of Mexico. The largest wilderness swamp in the nation, the Atchafalaya Basin, was created by all this water. Hundreds of species of birds stop there during their migrations. Fish fill its swamps, and reptiles and amphibians live in its tall cordgrass. The swamps are also home to threatened and **endangered** species, such as the Louisiana black bear, pallid sturgeon, and American alligator.

The southwestern part of the state has many remarkable landforms, such as barrier islands, marshes, grasslands, beaches, and cheniers—oak-covered islands formed from crushed shells and sand. Rare and endangered creatures, such as the piping plover and the Kemp's Ridley sea turtle, find refuge along these coastal areas. Herons, egrets, pelicans, eagles, and a host of other shorebirds are also found along the Louisiana coast. Going north, a traveler will pass through the Cajun Prairie, where once-treeless grasslands have been replaced by thousands of acres of rice fields and pastures. This farmland gives way to rolling hills dotted with pine trees. These hills stretch toward the northwest border of the state.

On a hot summer day, children cool off in a fountain in St. Tammany Parish in southeastern Louisiana.

10 KEY SITES ★ ★ ★

Audubon Aquarium

Audubon Zoo

French Quarter

1. Audubon Aquarium of the Americas

Located in New Orleans, this aquarium features animals from both North and South America. Visitors can see huge sharks, sea otters, sea turtles, and owls. You can even touch some stingrays.

2. Audubon Zoo

Also located in New Orleans, the Audubon Zoo covers 58 acres (23 ha) and features more than 2,000 animals. Some of the most popular exhibits are the elephants, orangutans, jaguars, and white alligators.

3. French Quarter

The French Quarter in New Orleans is the oldest neighborhood in the city. Many of its buildings date back to the early to mid-1700s. Visitors can see these buildings while riding one of the Quarter's historic streetcars. In Jackson Square, there are street performers, artists, and square donuts to eat.

4. Honey Island Swamp

The Honey Island Swamp, in Slidell, is one of the least-touched swamps in the United States. If you're feeling brave, you can take a tour of its 250 square miles (647 sq km) and see various birds, fish, and maybe even a jaguar.

5. Jean Lafitte National Historic Park and Preserve

This national park has six sites throughout the state. The Barataria Preserve, in Marrero, features a 23,000-acre (9,308 ha) wetland and visitor center. At Chalmette Battlefield you can learn about the Battle of New Orleans in the War of 1812. The park's four other sites feature tours, music, and exhibits.

6. Louisiana State Museum

The Louisiana State Museum is a series of historic landmarks and museums. At the Capitol Park Museum, in Baton Rouge, you can learn about the state's history and culture. The Louisiana Sports Hall of Fame & Northwest Louisiana History Museum in Natchitoches celebrates Louisiana athletes, coaches, and Northwest Louisiana.

7. National World War II Museum

Opened in 2000 as the National D-Day Museum, the National World War II Museum in New Orleans tells the story of America's participation in and contributions to the victory over Japan, Germany, and Italy.

8. New Orleans Museum of Art

The oldest fine arts museum in the city, the NOMA opened in 1911 with only nine works of art. Today, the museum features around 40,000 objects, including French and American art, photography, and glass.

9. Oak Valley Plantation

This historic plantation in Vacherie was built in 1837. Hundreds of slaves worked there between 1836 and the Civil War. Today, visitors can tour the mansion, walk the grounds, and learn about the history of slavery on the property.

10. USS *Kidd* Veterans Memorial

The USS *Kidd* is a U.S. Navy destroyer that served during WWII and the Korean War. Visitors can tour the ship, see artifacts, aircraft, and learn about the brave men and women who served their country.

Louisiana State Museum

New Orleans Museum of Art

USS *Kidd*

Spanish moss is a common sight hanging from trees in Louisiana.

Climate and Seasons

Louisiana's warm temperatures and steady rains make the state a year-round paradise for gardeners. But Louisianans must also deal with tornadoes, hurricanes, other wind and rain storms, and often extremely high humidity (the amount of moisture in the air).

Summers in Louisiana are long and hot. Winters are short and mild. In the northern city of Shreveport, the temperature typically stays above 90 degrees Fahrenheit (32 degrees Celsius) for most of the summer. The high humidity makes northern Louisiana steamy and uncomfortable in summer. During northern Louisiana's coolest month, January, temperatures are about 46°F (8 °C). Record-setting temperatures in the state have occurred in the north. On August 10, 1936, the temperature in Plain Dealing reached 114 °F (46 °C). Minden recorded the coldest temperature, −16 °F (−27 °C), back in February 1899.

The Gulf of Mexico creates a steadier climate for southern Louisiana. The gulf affects the winds and the air temperature, resulting in fewer extremes of hot and cold. Breezes from the gulf cool off the land in summer and warm it in winter. Summer temperatures in southern Louisiana average 84 °F (29 °C). The winter temperatures average about 55 °F (13 °C).

Wind and rain affect the entire state. Northern Louisiana is in the path of strong winds that blow across the Great Plains and is on the southern edge of a region known as "Tornado Alley." Spring is the most threatening time of year for thunderstorms, hailstorms, and tornadoes, as cold air from the Great Plains runs into warm air from the Gulf of Mexico. When the weather fronts **collide**, air begins to swirl and forms funnel clouds and hail. Summer brings unstable weather to southern Louisiana. Violent hurricanes batter the coast with raging winds, high surf, flooding, and heavy rain. The worst hurricane to hit the state was Hurricane Katrina, which struck in August 2005.

Hurricane Katrina caused such bad flooding that this chair ended up in a tree.

The Louisiana wetlands are a great spot for seeing migratory birds.

In Louisiana, precipitation usually falls in the form of rain. Yearly rainfall in Louisiana averages from 51 inches (130 centimeters) in the northwest to 66 inches (168 cm) in the southeast. Snow occasionally falls in the north. In winter, frost forms when polar air moves down from Alaska and Canada and settles over the state. From late fall to early spring, farmers must protect their crops from the effects of frost. The growing season is measured by the number of days between the last spring frost and the first fall frost. Farmers statewide enjoy very long growing seasons, up to 290 days in the south.

Louisiana Wildlife

As naturalist John Audubon noted, the variety of Louisiana's wildlife seems endless. Many types of trees, shrubs, and grasses thrive in the fields and marshes and along the coast. Wildflowers and other blooms fill the fields in the spring and summer. Deer, black bears, and red wolves live in the pine-filled woods, while catfish, bass, trout, crawfish, and alligators swim in the swamps and rivers. The state's coastal marshes, islands, and beaches are home to brown pelicans, nutria (a type of rodent), crappies (a type of fish), redear sunfish, and green tree frogs. An abundance of sea life, including oysters, rays, sharks, speckled trout, and bluefish, lives just offshore in the Gulf. Huge numbers of crabs and shrimp inhabit local waters, too. While many plants and animals can be found in abundance, concerned citizens throughout the state are acting to protect Louisiana's rare or endangered species. These include sea turtles, the Louisiana quillwort (a grasslike water plant), and birds such as the red-cockaded woodpecker, least tern, and piping plover.

Louisiana's life-giving rivers can also cause serious problems. Every summer, an area that scientists call a "dead zone" forms off the coast of Louisiana. As the Mississippi River flows past farms, it carries away some of the **fertilizers** that have been used on the farmland. When the river empties into the Gulf of Mexico, the fertilizers are deposited along the coast, contributing to a burst of algae growth. This causes a loss of oxygen in the water, and the low oxygen levels kill fish, shrimp, crabs, and other sea life. In recent summers, the size of the dead zone has been close to 8,000 square miles (20,700 sq km)—about the size of New Jersey. To try to fix the problem, people all along the Mississippi River are learning ways to keep fertilizers out of the water. They are building barriers and filters that help prevent fertilizers from spreading into rivers.

This satellite image shows the Gulf of Mexico dead zone off the coast of Louisiana.

American Alligator

Catfish

Live Oak

1. State Reptile: American Alligator

The American alligator lives in Louisiana's rivers, lakes, canals, and bayous. On average, they are 13 feet (4 m) long and weigh 450 to 600 pounds (200–270 kg). Alligators eat fish, turtles, snails, and small mammals.

2. State Tree: Bald Cypress

The bald cypress became Louisiana's state tree in 1963. The wood from the bald cypress is very heavy and strong. It is often used in construction and to build furniture.

3. Catfish

Blue, flathead, channel, and hardhead catfish are found in some of Louisiana's freshwater lakes, ponds, and rivers. The blue catfish is the largest in North America. It can weigh more than 100 pounds (45 kg).

4. State Crustacean: Crawfish

Louisiana supplies around 95 percent of the crawfish harvested in the United States. They are a very popular food source. Crawfish are often boiled, fried, and used in soups and stews. They are known for soaking up the flavors of seasonings and spices, so crawfish can be sweet, savory, or spicy!

5. Live Oak

Live oaks got their name because they grow new leaves as soon as the old ones die. Reaching heights of 40 to 50 feet (12–15 m), the tree's wood is very dense and was once used for shipbuilding. Many animals, such as wild turkeys, foxes, rabbits, and black bears, rely on the acorns of live oaks for food.

6. State Mammal: Louisiana Black Bear

The Louisiana black bear became the state mammal in 1992. The Louisiana black bear is different from other black bears in that its skull is longer and thinner. Living in swampy forests, the black bear eats mostly berries and acorns.

7. State Flower: Magnolia

The magnolia became Louisiana's state flower in 1900. Its large, fragrant flowers make it a beautiful decoration that is seen throughout the state. Squirrels, opossums, and turkeys eat the magnolia's seeds. Wood from the magnolia tree is used to make furniture.

8. Snowy Egret

Snowy egrets nest near Louisiana's swamps. The birds are 20 to 40 inches (50–100 cm) tall, with long black legs, yellow toes, black bills, and white feathers. During the mating season, snowy egrets will grow wispy plumes of long, white feathers.

9. Spanish Moss

Spanish moss grows on trees. It is not actually a moss, however. It is an epiphyto, which means it grows on other plants for support. Fragrant, tiny flowers burst forth from the moss in spring.

10. Western Cottonmouth Snake

This dark-colored snake lives near water and is a very poisonous member of the pit viper family. While waiting to attack small animals, a cottonmouth lies coiled with its head flung back and its cotton-colored mouth wide open. Once it finds its food, the snake strikes quickly and snaps shut its powerful jaws.

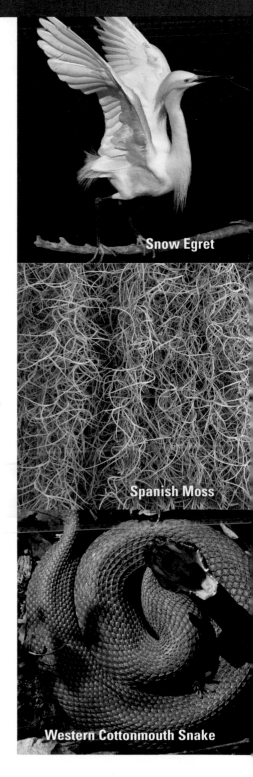
Snow Egret

Spanish Moss

Western Cottonmouth Snake

Louisiana was claimed for France by René-Robert Cavelier, sieur de La Salle in 1682.

From the Beginning

Louisiana's past is as complex and shifting as the Mississippi River flowing across its land. From ancient Native American artists to Caribbean **pirates**, from French-Acadian **refugees** to African-American jazz musicians, Louisiana is a state with a people and history like no other.

The First People

Prehistoric groups of people first arrived in present-day Louisiana during the last ice age, about 10,000 BCE. It was a much cooler and drier place then. These people were **nomadic** hunters, meaning they followed their food from place to place. As early as 3400 BCE, some built extraordinary mounds of earth. In northern Louisiana, in an area called Watson Brake, scientists have discovered eleven huge mounds that rise up to 25 feet (8 m). Scientists are still puzzled by the purpose of the mounds.

In addition to hunting, the prehistoric people fished in the rivers and gathered fruits and nuts. Scientists refer to these tribes as the Mound Builders. In later years, the descendants of Mound Builders used tools, worked metal, and decorated pottery. Some began to stay in one place year-round. They traded with tribes as far away as present-day Wisconsin.

The people who met the European explorers in the sixteenth century were descendants of the Mound Builders. These Native Americans lived along the coast and waterways of southeastern Louisiana. Most were farmers who tended crops of maize, melons, squash,

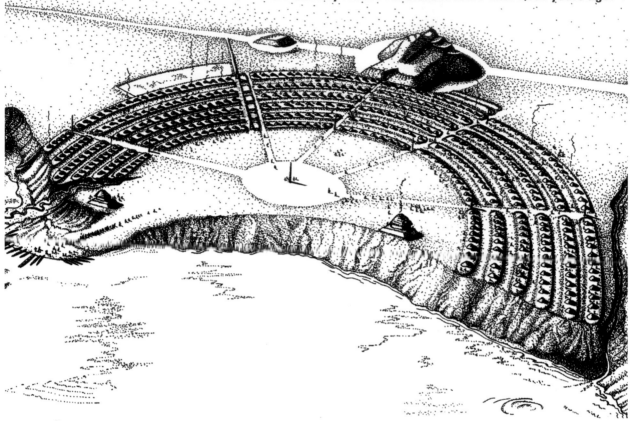

This illustration shows the complex layout of the earthen mounds and terraces at Poverty Point in northern Louisiana. The mounds were built by Native Americans more than 3,000 years ago.

beans, and millet—a type of grain. Men hunted bear, rabbit, deer, and wild turkeys with bows and arrows. But the major sources of food for southern groups were fish, clams, and oysters.

Their villages were groups of homes made from poles and thatched leaves. For transportation, the Native Americans built dugout canoes from trees. People wore dyed and painted clothing made from animal skins. Both men and women wore jewelry— anklets, earrings, necklaces, and nose rings. Men and women also wore tattoos that symbolized their achievements in life.

Many different tribes lived across Louisiana. Most belonged to one of six major cultural groups. The Tunica and Natchez culture groups were found in the northeast. People who spoke the Muskogean language lived in the central regions. These included the Natchez, Houma, and Choctaw tribes. The Caddo, including the Natchitoches, lived in the northwest. The Chitimacha and Attakapa peoples lived along the coast and swamps of the southwest.

European Encounters

In 1519, a Spanish explorer, Alvarez de Pineda, traveled through the region and reported seeing a river flowing with gold. What he probably saw was the Mississippi River. Another Spanish explorer, Hernando de Soto, undoubtedly explored the Mississippi in 1541. de Soto led an expedition for gold through much of America's southeast. However, he died before his army entered Louisiana. The Europeans brought diseases that quickly spread among the native population. Many died before the next major contact with European explorers.

In 1682, French explorer René-Robert Cavelier, sieur de La Salle, traveled down the Mississippi River. He claimed the area that now includes Louisiana and some of the neighboring states for the French king, Louis XIV. La Salle named the territory Louisiane in honor of the king.

After La Salle's claim, Pierre and Jean-Baptiste Le Moyne set sail from France and founded an outpost near present-day Biloxi, Mississippi, in 1699. The settlers encountered Native Americans and built forts to protect themselves from the Spanish, who had settled in present-day Florida and Mexico, and the British, who had established colonies along the continent's east coast.

In Their Own Words

"I became totally intrigued with Louisiana—the people, the food. It is a part of my life. Everything that has happened for me since moving here has just been icing on the cake."
—Emeril Lagasse, chef and restaurateur

This painting shows La Salle's expedition arriving at the mouth of the Mississippi River in 1682.

The Native People

When French settlers first started exploring Louisiana, they discovered that a variety of people already lived there. The state had more than 10,000 indigenous people living in different tribes. Settlement of the Louisiana region dates back as far as 10,000 years ago, and farming of the land began 2,000 years ago. Along the Gulf Coast, the Atakapa lived in the western side of the state, while the Chitimachu lived on the eastern Gulf coast. The Caddo people were located in the western and northern sections of what is now Louisiana, and the eastern portion of the land was populated by the Tunica, Natchez, Houma, and Choctaw people. The Choctaw was one of the largest and most dispersed tribes in Louisiana.

While these tribes had different languages and customs, there were also striking similarities between the groups. Most tribes hunted, fished, and farmed. Homes were constructed from tree branches, grasses, and wattle and daub. Almost all tribes had faiths based on the spirituality of nature, and many indigenous people honored their dead with burial mounds.

The Europeans that came to the area borrowed many of the tools Louisiana Natives used, including dugout canoes, baskets made of river cane, blowguns, and more. When the Europeans sought to drive out or assimilate the Natives of the state, many used the area swamps to hide. The United States used some treaties to take land from the Natives, but also forced many to cede their lands and then relocate to what is now Oklahoma. This was called the Trail of Tears, during which 2,500 Native Americans died. Over time, some Louisiana Natives made their way back to the state and rebuilt their lives. Some tribes continue to speak their original languages to this day.

Today, there are four federally recognized tribes in Louisiana, including the Chitimacha Tribe of Louisiana, the Coushatta Tribe of Louisiana, the Jena Band of Choctaw, and the Tunica-Biloxi Tribe of Louisiana. In addition, the state itself recognizes ten tribes, including the Addai Caddo Tribe, the Biloxi-Chitimacha Confederation of Muskogee, the Choctaw-Apache Community of Ebarb, the Clifton Choctaw, the Four Winds Tribe Louisiana Cherokee Confederacy, the Grand Caillou/Dulac Band, the Isle de Jean Charles Band, the Louisiana Choctaw Tribe, the Point-Au-Chien Tribe, and the United Houma Nation.

Spotlight on the Choctaw

The Choctaw are descendants of the Muskogean people, a mound-building society that lived in the Mississippi River Valley for more than 1,000 years before the Europeans arrived.

This painting shows Choctaw people playing a traditional game in which they use rackets and tall goalposts. Sometimes hundreds of people played at once.

Clans: Within the Choctaw tribe there were two groups: the elders and the youth. Both groups had several clans, called Iskas. A child was born into the Iska to which his or her mother belonged. Fathers had limited control over their children. In Choctaw society, a child's oldest maternal uncle looked after him or her.

Homes: Choctaw winter houses were circular, made with wood frames, and covered with mud. The roofs were made from tree bark and grasses. Summer houses were rectangular, with two holes on either end that let air flow in and out easily.

Food: The Choctaw were excellent farmers. Corn was their main crop, but they also grew other vegetables. Men hunted deer, turkeys, rabbits, and other small animals.

Clothing: Early female Choctaw clothing consisted of blouses and short skirts made of animal hide. Men wore breechcloths (loincloths), and both men and women often went barefoot at home. In later days, women wore blouses and skirts made of cotton material. Both men and women wore their hair long.

Art: The Choctaw were known for making beautiful baskets. They were made with river cane and palmetto grass, and then dyed with plant dye. These baskets were used in food preparation, storage, and given as gifts.

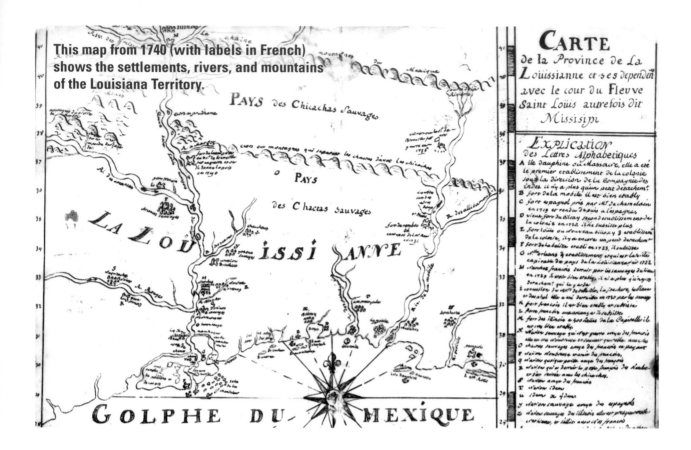

This map from 1740 (with labels in French) shows the settlements, rivers, and mountains of the Louisiana Territory.

Meanwhile in Europe, France, Spain, and their allies were at war with Great Britain and its allies. France needed money to support the war effort. Louisiana was not a moneymaking colony for France, so the French government decided to turn it over to private funders. The first permanent settlement was founded in 1714 at present-day Natchitoches. From 1717 to 1731, a Scottish economist named John Law convinced thousands of people to come to Louisiana. Investors in France funded the settlements. Some settlers were prisoners shipped out of France by government officials who did not want these criminals in France. Others were Europeans who were promised land and livestock in exchange for settlement. So many Germans accepted Law's offer that the Mississippi shoreline west of New Orleans became known as the German Coast.

Law promised riches, but the pioneers found the land to be an insect-filled swamp full of deadly tropical diseases and a native population unhappy about the newcomers' arrival.

More than 5,000 slaves from West Africa and the French-owned Caribbean islands arrived during that period, too. In addition to working against their will, the slaves suffered from the intense heat, insects, and disease. But they brought valuable farming knowledge to the land. Tobacco and **indigo** became cash crops. Yet farming settlements did not make anyone wealthy. The investors stopped paying, and Law's company eventually went **bankrupt**.

Meanwhile, the Spanish built Fort Los Adaes in northwestern Louisiana. It became the capital of Texas Province in 1729. As European settlements grew and prospered, the colonists took over more and more of the land belonging to the native people. Many tribes had to fend for themselves or pick a European nation to befriend. Both the Natchez and the Chickasaw groups fought the French. However, the Choctaw stood by the French in many conflicts.

In the mid–1750s, most European powers, including France, were again at war. In North America, the war between France and Great Britain was called the French and Indian War. Many battles were fought on North American soil. By 1762, the French sensed defeat. They did not want to lose their territory to the British. Instead, France gave all its land west of the Mississippi River, plus New Orleans, to its ally Spain. When the war ended in 1763, France surrendered the remainder of its North American territory to Great Britain.

The Founder of New Orleans

Jean-Baptiste Le Moyne was 18 when he helped his brother settle the first colony in the Louisiana Territory. Two years later, he was appointed governor of the territory. In the 1720s, he helped pick the site for New Orleans and named it for Philippe II, Duke of Orleans, who in effect ruled France at the time [because the king was still a child]. The city became the capital of the territory in 1723.

Making a Mardi Gras Bead Necklace

People celebrate Mardi Gras by dressing in costumes and masks. They also wear bright, colorful beads. Throwing beads from parade floats has been a Mardi Gras tradition since the 1920s. Follow these instructions to make your own Mardi Gras bead necklace.

What You Need

Pasta with holes

Purple, green, and gold paint

Paint brush

Tape

Yarn

Safety scissors

What To Do

• Sort the pasta into three groups and paint each group a different color.

• Let the pasta dry.

• Size the yarn to your desired length and cut to size (with the help of an adult).

• Tape one end of your yarn to the table.

• Take each piece of pasta and thread the yarn through them, taking turns with each color.

• When you've reached the end of the yarn, tie a knot.

• Now you are ready for Mardi Gras!

By that time, the first of thousands of French colonists had begun to arrive from Canada. The Acadians had lived on the island of Nova Scotia in eastern Canada for more than a century. In 1755, the British demanded that the Acadians sign a loyalty oath to Great Britain.

When the Acadians refused, the British forced them out. Many Acadians traveled thousands of miles to reach the former French colony of Louisiana. There, the Acadian refugees later became known as Cajuns.

American Revolution

In 1775, the thirteen British colonies along the east coast of America began their fight for independence. The Spanish governor of Louisiana helped the colonists. He allowed goods to travel up the Mississippi River to supply the American revolutionaries. In 1783, the colonies won their independence and became the United States of America. Through a deal with Spain, New Orleans became an important port city for the newly independent nation.

In 1800, Spain signed a treaty that returned the huge Louisiana Territory to France. The area included all or part of fourteen future U.S. states, not just Louisiana. U.S. president Thomas Jefferson worried that France would close New Orleans to American shipping. The United States offered to buy the territory. At the time, French emperor Napoleon Bonaparte was leading a military campaign through Europe. In 1803, to raise money, he sold the entire Louisiana Territory for $15 million. This sale, known as the Louisiana Purchase, greatly increased the size of the United States. To make governing the region easier, the territory was divided. One part was called the Territory of Orleans. This area included most of present-day Louisiana.

Pirates and Generals

By 1810, the future state's population grew to more than 76,000 people. New steam-powered ships began traveling the Mississippi River, carrying tons of goods and supplies to and from the expanding nation. New Orleans became the seventh-largest city in the United States. On April 30, 1812, Louisiana became the eighteenth state.

This illustration shows General Andrew Jackson's army, including black soldiers, fighting during the Battle of New Orleans in January 1815.

In the early 1800s, pirates were operating in the Caribbean Sea. Many brought stolen goods to New Orleans to sell. Some pirates, known as privateers, were given permission by the United States to attack any non-American ship. The British began fighting the privateers, but they also started kidnapping American sailors and invading American waters. In response, the United States declared war on Great Britain in 1812.

During the War of 1812, British generals saw the importance of New Orleans as a seaport and planned an attack. They invited one of the most notorious pirates, Jean Lafitte, to join their navy. But Louisiana's governor ordered a raid on Lafitte's harbor at Barataria Bay and captured his brother Pierre. Meanwhile, American General Andrew Jackson prepared to defend the city with whoever was willing to fight, including free blacks and Choctaw warriors. Jean Lafitte gathered other pirates to help Jackson's troops in return for Pierre's freedom. On January 8, 1815, General Jackson's motley army defeated a British force that was twice its size. What came to be known as the Battle of New Orleans was a great victory. Little did the opposing armies know that two weeks earlier the United States and Great Britain had signed a treaty that ended the war. Andrew Jackson became a national hero and was elected president of the United States in 1828.

This photo from the 1800s shows Oak Alley, a plantation along the Mississippi River. Plantations such as this were common in the South, and many of them used slave labor.

★ 10 ★ KEY CITIES ★ ★ ★

New Orleans

Baton Rouge

Shreveport

1. New Orleans: population 343,829

New Orleans is known as one of the most interesting cities in the world. Because of its history, the city's food, music, and dance are influenced by Caribbean, European, and African culture. You can stroll through the historic French Quarter, eat delicious food, such as gumbo, and listen to jazz.

2. Baton Rouge: population 229,493

Baton Rouge is the farthest inland deep-water port on the Mississippi River. Therefore, it sees a lot of commercial and industrial activity. With four colleges located there, around 20 percent of Baton Rouge's population is made up of students.

3. Shreveport: population 199,311

Located in western Louisiana near the Texas border, Shreveport is known for its riverboat casinos on the Red River. Visitors also enjoy the city's parks, waterfront dining, shopping, and entertainment.

4. Lafayette: population 120,623

Lafayette is the center of Cajun culture in Louisiana and the United States. This makes the city a popular place for tourists. Food markets, concerts, and street festivals are just some of the activities that residents and visitors enjoy there.

5. Lake Charles: population 71,993

Nicknamed "The Festival Capital of Louisiana," Lake Charles hosts more than 75 festivals each year. One of them, called Contraband Days, is a two week-long celebration that honors the pirates who once sailed Lake Charles and are said to have buried their contraband, or loot, there.

6. Kenner: population 66,702

Kenner is a suburb of New Orleans, located northwest of the city. Among Kenner's attractions is Rivertown, a historic district located on the city's original main street. It features shops, museums, theaters, and restaurants.

7. Bossier City: population 61,315

Bossier City is located across the Red River from Shreveport. Therefore, it shares the riverboat casinos with its neighbor. Bossier City also has a horse racetrack, parks, dining, and outlet shopping.

8. Monroe: population 48,815

Monroe is home to the Louisiana Purchase Gardens and Zoo, which features more than 500 animals. The city also has several museums, including the Louisiana Children's Museum, the Biedenharn Museum and Gardens, and the Chennault Aviation and Military Museum.

9. Alexandria: population 47,723

Alexandria sits in the center of Louisiana. The city has become a popular place to raise a family. Alexandria's economy has been steady, and *National Geographic Traveler* magazine ranked it as one of America's top ten "wilderness towns," because of the nearby national forests.

10. Houma: population 33,727

Houma was named after the historic Houma Native American tribe that lived, and continues to live, there. The Houma area has around 2,500 square miles (6,475 sq km) of swamps and wetlands, which are popular places to tour and go fishing.

Bossier City

Monroe

Alexandria

A Growing Economy

Large Louisiana farms, or plantations, became very profitable in the first half of the nineteenth century. Cotton grew well in the northern part of the state, and sugar thrived in the south. White landowners operated the plantations and used black slaves to perform the hard labor of planting and harvesting crops. Some white landowners grew wealthy as a result of slave labor and the ease with which they could ship their crops up and down the Mississippi River. One of these people was Zachary Taylor. He made Baton Rouge his adopted home before being elected U.S. president in 1848. A year later, the city became the capital of Louisiana.

New Orleans thrived as the second-busiest port in the United States. From 1820 to 1860, hundreds of thousands of **immigrants** arrived from Europe, South America, and the Caribbean. The city had more free blacks than any other city in the United States. Life became a mix of many cultures. In 1843, the University of Louisiana (later renamed Tulane University) was founded in the city.

The War Between the States

Slavery was a major topic of debate in the United States in the first half of the nineteenth century. Most people living in Northern states wanted to abolish, or end, slavery. But Southern states relied on slavery to support their economy.

In 1860, Abraham Lincoln, an antislavery politician, was elected president. South Carolina decided to secede, or withdraw, from the United States (the Union). Louisiana was one of ten other Southern states that, in 1861, also seceded. These states formed the Confederate States of America. Lincoln refused to accept the withdrawal of these Southern states from the Union.

In April 1861, Confederate soldiers fired on and captured Fort Sumter in South Carolina. It was the start of the Civil War, which would continue for four years.

Few battles took place within Louisiana. Early in the war, Union troops occupied New Orleans and Baton Rouge, taking control of the ports and most of the lower Mississippi River boat traffic. The Union army declared New Orleans the capital of all the Union-controlled land in Louisiana. Louisiana's Confederate government moved its capital from

Baton Rouge to Shreveport. Thousands of escaped slaves joined the Union army. Many were organized into regiments to defend New Orleans and other key cities. The Confederacy eventually lost the war. In April 1865, Confederate General Robert E. Lee surrendered to Union General Ulysses S. Grant. Later that year, Louisiana was one of thirty states that approved the Thirteenth Amendment to the U.S. Constitution, which abolished slavery in the United States.

The First African-American Newspaper

The New Orleans Tribune was the first black-run daily newspaper in the nation. It started in 1864 and was only one two-sided piece of paper. The front was written in French, the language of many newly freed slaves. The back was in English, which was spoken by most free blacks.

African-American Union soldiers fought bravely during the Battle of Fort Hudson, Louisiana, in May 1863.

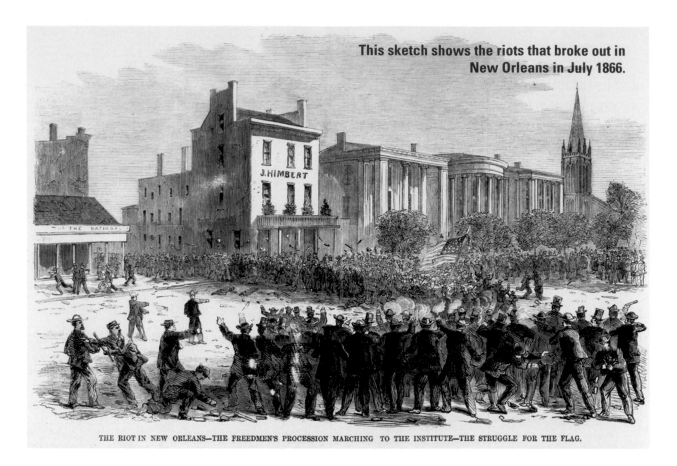

THE RIOT IN NEW ORLEANS—THE FREEDMEN'S PROCESSION MARCHING TO THE INSTITUTE—THE STRUGGLE FOR THE FLAG.

The Reconstruction Era and Beyond

Louisiana was a different place after the Civil War. Crops and farms were ruined, homes were destroyed, schools were empty, roads were unusable, and banks and other businesses failed. Angry at the loss of their old way of life, many Southerners resented Northerners who came to the South. They called them "carpetbaggers," because their traveling bags were made from carpets.

Though slaves were now free, Louisiana and other Southern states passed new laws known as Black Codes. These codes took away many of the rights promised to African Americans, such as the freedom to have certain jobs or live in certain places. In July 1866, a group of politicians met in New Orleans to discuss issues including voting rights. A crowd of white people, including police officers, killed more than thirty black people and several of their white supporters.

This incident and other events led the U.S. Congress to pass the first of several laws called the Reconstruction Acts. The acts put the former Confederate states under U.S. Army control. Like the other states, Louisiana could not return to the Union as a state without drafting and accepting a new state constitution. Louisiana citizens adopted a new constitution that gave some rights to members of all races and voting rights to black men. The constitution also called for at least one public school in every parish. All children ages six to eighteen could attend, no matter the color of their skin. On June 25, 1868, Louisiana was officially readmitted as a state.

Louisiana during this time took bold steps forward and suffered violent reactions. John W. Menard was the first African American elected to Congress. But the 1868 election results were disputed, and he was never seated. In 1872, P. B. S. Pinchback briefly served as governor, the first African American to hold that office. Some white Louisianans fought such changes with intimidation and violence. They joined organizations such as the White League and the Ku Klux Klan. These groups terrorized African Americans and the whites who supported equal opportunities for African Americans.

In 1877, federal control of Reconstruction ended in Louisiana. The army left and new politicians came into power. They did very little to help Louisianans because they believed that was not the government's role. Much of the progress made during Reconstruction was stopped.

Life in the countryside remained difficult. Many people found jobs mining sulfur or salt or harvesting pine and cypress for lumber. More than sixty towns grew around lumber companies in Louisiana. Other towns grew along the newly built railroads that ran through the delta. Farmers from the Northeast and Midwest produced an abundance of rice in the prairies of southwest Louisiana.

However, many more landowners could not afford to run their plantations now that slaves no longer provided free labor. The solution was a system called sharecropping. Black and white farm laborers worked a portion of the land and gave a percentage of their earnings to the landowner. Usually money did not exchange hands. Instead, landowners would provide the sharecroppers with tools, food, and supplies on credit during the planting and growing seasons. When it was time to split the earnings after crops were harvested, most of the sharecroppers' portion went to the landowner to pay off the loans. Many former slaves found themselves working the same land and living in the same houses as they had before they were free.

By the end of the nineteenth century, nearly all the rights granted to African-American citizens in Louisiana had been taken away. White politicians who controlled the government passed many "Jim Crow" laws. These laws called for separation of the races in schools, in public places, and in public transportation. In 1892, a group of black leaders in New Orleans decided to challenge the laws. Homer Plessy, a shoemaker of black descent,

By the late 1800s, steam excavators were used in the exhausting work of sulfur mining.

boarded a whites-only train car and was arrested. The case went all the way to the U.S. Supreme Court. The Court ruled that segregation laws were legal as long as they provided for "equal" service to blacks and whites. The decision was a major blow to African Americans in their struggle for equal rights.

In 1898, a new state constitution required that black men must own property, be able to read and write, and pay a fee (called a poll tax) before they could vote. However, white men did not need to meet these requirements to vote. (At the time, no women were allowed to vote.) It would be many years before black Louisianans were given equal rights.

The 1900s

The new century brought a new industry—**petroleum**. After oil was found near Jennings in 1901, oil wells sprang up across the southern part of the state and later in the northwest near Shreveport and Bossier City. Pipelines were built to send oil from fields in Texas and Oklahoma to the port at Baton Rouge.

In 1927, heavy rains caused weeks of flooding along the banks of the Mississippi River between Missouri and the Gulf of Mexico. In Louisiana, the water broke through the levees that landowners had built in the lowlands. The river rose nearly 50 feet (15 m) at

 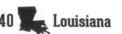

Baton Rouge. Hundreds of thousands of people were left homeless, and millions of dollars worth of property was destroyed.

In 1928, Huey P. Long was elected governor of Louisiana. A year later, the United States entered a period of severe economic hardship known as the Great Depression. Millions of Americans were out of work. Long created jobs for Louisiana farmers who could not find employment elsewhere. They worked on large public improvement projects, such as roads, schools, and flood-control programs. Long taxed wealthy citizens and large corporations and used the money to run social programs, such as providing free textbooks to public school students.

When the United States entered World War II in 1941, Louisiana farmers and factory workers provided much-needed supplies. The state was rich with oil and minerals that were important to the war effort. For the first time in the state's history, there were more citizens working in the cities than in rural areas. Baton Rouge nearly quadrupled in size. While men were fighting overseas, women worked in factories and in other jobs that used to be off-limits to them. The shipyards in New Orleans built many vessels for use in the war. After the war, the boom times in the cities continued. New tax laws invited more and more industry to the state.

Circumstances also started to improve for African Americans. The U.S. Supreme Court ruled in 1954 on a case that started in Kansas, called *Brown v. Board of Education of Topeka*. The Court overturned the earlier decision in Homer Plessy's case and said that it was not possible to have separate but equal schools for black children and white children. All schools had to be open to children of all races. Although the 1954 decision applied only to schools, it was an important legal step toward ending many other types of segregation—for example, on buses and trains, and in restaurants and other public places. Change did not come right away. But the 1954 decision gave hope to black citizens, who would see many of their civil rights restored over the next decades.

A Century Closes

Louisiana enjoyed decades of prosperity after World War II. Oil provided a lot of money and jobs for the state. But in the 1980s, oil prices declined around the world, and Louisiana went into another depression. To try to regain lost income, the state looked to its unique heritage. The government promoted tourism in the state. It also changed its gambling laws to allow riverboat casinos to open near New Orleans, Baton Rouge, Lake Charles, and Shreveport. From 1994 to 1999, tourism grew more in Louisiana than in any other state.

Billions of dollars in increased income earned from tourism and gambling helped the state in many ways. One area was the improvement of the public school system. In the late 1990s, Louisiana began repairing or replacing aged school buildings and raised teachers' salaries.

Hurricane Katrina and Recovery

Tragedy struck on August 29, 2005, when Hurricane Katrina raged over southeast Louisiana. Rain and strong winds created huge ocean waves that pounded New Orleans. Water levels rose in Lake Pontchartrain, just north of New Orleans, pouring water over the city's levees. Eventually some levees broke. Four-fifths of New Orleans was flooded. The southeast section called the Lower Ninth Ward and nearby St. Bernard Parish were almost entirely underwater.

About 1,500 people died. Around 900,000 lost their homes. Thousands flocked to shelters set up in the Superdome, the city's convention center, and other places, where they waited for days for any kind of assistance. Clean drinking water and food were hard to find. The government was slow to provide relief. After help arrived, some people settled in nearby cities, but a quarter of New Orleanians left for Texas and other neighboring states. Many people never came back.

Cleanup required a lot of hard work. The leftover **debris** could have filled the Superdome thirteen times. People from across the nation and the world came to help Louisiana, and residents began rebuilding levees, schools, other public buildings, and homes. In a matter of years, New Orleans became one of America's fastest-growing cities. Still, that was growth from a very low starting point, and it may be many years before the population of New Orleans returns to its pre-Katrina level.

★ 10 KEY ★ DATES IN STATE HISTORY

 1. 3400 BCE
Early inhabitants of modern-day Louisiana, the Mound Builders, make large hills at Watson Brake. The hills form a circle, and they range from 3 feet to 25 feet high.

 2. Spring 1682
René-Robert Cavelier, sieur de La Salle, explores the Mississippi River and claims a huge area of land for King Louis XIV of France.

 3. April 30, 1803
France sells the Louisiana Territory to the United States in the Louisiana Purchase. In total, the U.S. purchases around 827,000 square miles (2,141,920 sq km) of land west of the Mississippi River.

 4. April 30, 1812
Louisiana becomes the 18th state to enter the Union. Politician William Charles Cole Claiborne becomes the first governor.

 5. January 26, 1861
Louisiana secedes from the United States and joins the Confederacy. At this time, around 47 percent of the population is enslaved. Several months later, in April, the Civil War begins with the Confederate capture of South Carolina's Fort Sumter.

 6. June 25, 1868
Louisiana is officially readmitted to the United States as a state during a time called "Reconstruction," during which the country rebuilds itself after the war.

 7. September 21, 1901
After word that oil is present, a well near Jennings produces oil for the first time. By the end of 1905, more than 6 million barrels of oil are produced from it.

 8. August 29, 2005
Hurricane Katrina makes landfall in Louisiana. Levees meant to protect the city break under the weight of the water. Around four-fifths of the city is flooded.

 9. April 20, 2010
The Deepwater Horizon, an offshore oil drilling rig owned by oil company BP, explodes. The accident kills 11 people and spills 210 million gallons (795 million liters) of oil into the Gulf of Mexico. Around 125 miles (201 km) of Louisiana coastline is polluted.

 10. 2013
Balls of tar and oil are still found in the water and on Louisiana's beaches. Louisiana is the only state in which cleanup efforts are still taking place.

Purple, green, and gold are known as **Mardi Gras** colors. Purple represents justice, green represents faith, and gold represents power.

The People

Ever since French colonists settled alongside native tribes, Louisiana has been a land of many traditions. The Native Americans taught the European settlers many secrets to survival. These included which vegetables to grow, how to cook with native herbs and spices, where to fish and trap, and how to navigate the winding waterways by canoe. By the early eighteenth century, however, life was different. European diseases and violence between the tribes and colonists destroyed much of the native population. The Native Americans who survived moved to remote communities in the region or west to new territories. Today in Louisiana, there are only four small reservations for Native Americans that are recognized by the federal government.

However, Native American influence can be seen in hundreds of place names, such as Atchafalaya, Natchitoches, and Kisatchie. The word bayou comes from the Choctaw word bayuk, which means "small stream." Another sign of indigenous traditions in Louisiana culture is lagniappe (pronounced LAN-yap). In Louisiana, lagniappe is a little something extra that a shopkeeper or waiter sometimes gives a customer without charging for it. The Spanish picked up the word yapa from the Incas of South America, who used the word yapa to describe a little bonus given when trading. Many Louisianans believe lagniappe

Members of the Coushatta tribe take part in the National Powwow in Washington, D.C. The Coushatta are a federally-recognized tribe in Louisiana.

Tough Times

Disease and death were common in New Orleans in the 1800s. More than 12,000 people died of yellow fever during the summer of 1853 alone. Most people were buried in above-ground tombs because floods would simply raise coffins out of the earth.

encourages goodwill and friendship.

The Spanish followed the French into Louisiana. Together, the two European groups built a culture that came to be known as Creole, from a Spanish word for people of mixed backgrounds. Wealthy French and Spanish nobles moved to Louisiana and brought European-style art, music, and theater. They built gardens, parks, plantation manors, elegant townhomes, symphony and opera halls, and museums. To be Creole in the early days of the colony meant to be born in Louisiana of only Spanish and French heritage. But as Europeans, Native Americans, and African Americans intermarried, being Creole came to mean a person born in Louisiana who had a mixture of French, Spanish, and other backgrounds. Some people still speak a Creole version of French.

Many blacks arrived in Louisiana from West Africa as slaves in the late 1600s and early 1700s. Others came from Caribbean islands as free persons of color. Free people of color were often skilled artisans, such as the blacksmiths who created the ironwork that adorns buildings throughout the state. Some were highly educated. The Africans who arrived as slaves also brought customs and beliefs from their native cultures. At the time, the area was still under French law, which declared Sundays and religious holidays to be days of rest—even for slaves. On Sundays and holidays, Africans gathered in public and private meeting places. They sold food they had grown and crafts they had made. They practiced West African religious rituals and enjoyed the music, storytelling, and dance of their homelands. Congo Square in present-day Louis Armstrong Park in New Orleans is one such former public gathering place. Many music scholars believe Congo Square was where the musical style known as jazz was first heard.

In the early part of the eighteenth century, German farmers settled along the Mississippi River. French Acadians arrived later in the century, followed by people from the French Caribbean colony of Saint-Domingue (now the country of Haiti). Spanish-speaking people from the Canary Islands (located between Africa and Spain), called Isleños, settled in St. Bernard and Plaquemines parishes. Irish, English, and Scottish immigrants began arriving from the Appalachian region. At the end of the nineteenth century, Italians, most from Sicily, immigrated to Louisiana, first to farm and later to work in other businesses.

A band of drummers leads a parade through Congo Square in Louis Armstrong Park in New Orleans.

10 KEY PEOPLE ★ ★

Louis Armstrong

Michael DeBakey

Hunter Hayes

1. Louis Armstrong

Born in New Orleans in 1901, Louis Armstrong was one of the greatest jazz musicians in history. At age 13, he sang in the streets and then learned to play the trumpet. By 1930, he led his own band and performed around the world.

2. Michael DeBakey

Michael DeBakey was born in 1908 in Lake Charles. He developed several devices and techniques for heart surgery, and mobile army surgical hospital (MASH) units. In 1966, he performed the first successful transplant of a partial artificial heart.

3. Ellen DeGeneres

Ellen DeGeneres was born in 1958 in Metairie. She had a tough childhood, but she always kept her sense of humor. In 1984, DeGeneres won a televised search for the "Funniest Person in America." Since then, she has starred in two sitcoms and hosts her own talk show.

4. Hunter Hayes

Born in Breaux Bridge in 1991, Hayes has been making music since he was a toddler. He learned to play the guitar at age six, performed on TV, and signed a record deal in 2010. A year later, he released his first major label album, on which he co-wrote every song and played every instrument.

5. Mahalia Jackson

Mahalia Jackson was born in New Orleans in 1911. Jackson began singing at age four. While working as a maid, she sang in a choir. Soon Jackson was singing throughout the country. Jackson made dozens of influential gospel recordings and performed for audiences around the world.

LOUISIANA

 6. Randy Jackson

Born in Baton Rouge in 1956, Randy Jackson began playing bass guitar at age 13. He studied music in college, after which he became a record producer. Jackson went on to become a judge on *American Idol* from 2002 to 2013.

 7. Peyton and Eli Manning

The Manning brothers were star quarterbacks at their New Orleans high school. They both went on to the NFL. Peyton led the Indianapolis Colts to a Super Bowl win in 2007. Eli and the New York Giants won the Super Bowl in 2008 and 2012.

 8. Tyler Perry

Born Emmitt Perry, Jr. in New Orleans in 1969, Perry is an actor, author, playwright, producer, and director. After a tough childhood, Perry began writing. He wrote plays, movies, produced them, and even starred in some of them. Perry has become one of the most successful stars in Hollywood.

 9. Anne Rice

Anne Rice was born in New Orleans in 1941. After moving to California, Rice began writing. In 1976, her novel *Interview with the Vampire* became a huge success, and it was made into a movie in 1996. Since then, Rice's books have sold around 100 million copies.

 10. Britney Spears

Britney Spears is one of the biggest pop stars in history. Raised in Kentwood, Spears began performing as a young child. She appeared on *The All-New Mickey Mouse Club*, and she released her first album in 1999. Spears has sold more than 100 million albums worldwide.

Peyton and Eli Manning

Tyler Perry

Anne Rice

Who Louisianans Are

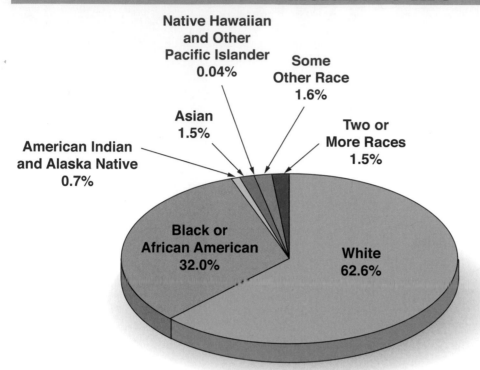

Native Hawaiian and Other Pacific Islander
0.04%

Some Other Race
1.6%

Asian
1.5%

American Indian and Alaska Native
0.7%

Two or More Races
1.5%

Black or African American
32.0%

White
62.6%

Total Population
4,533,372

Hispanic or Latino (of any race):

• 192,560 people (4.2%)

Note: The pie chart shows the racial breakdown of the state's population based on the categories used by the U.S. Bureau of the Census. The Census Bureau reports information for Hispanics or Latinos separately, since they may be of any race. Percentages in the pie chart may not total 100 because of rounding. Source: U.S. Bureau of the Census, 2010 Census

In the twentieth century, immigrants arrived from Latin America and Asia. Louisiana had long had a Hispanic population from the Canary Islands or other former Spanish colonies. But many newer arrivals come from Mexico. The largest Asian population has come from Vietnam. In the 1970s, during and after the Vietnam War, Catholic churches throughout the state sponsored Vietnamese refugees. Many came to Louisiana to start new lives. Some who had fished and caught shrimp in Asia found the same jobs there. In the twenty-first century, Vietnamese immigration to Louisiana has slowed, but thousands of new residents have come from India, China, and the Philippines.

Life in the North

Louisiana is often separated into north and south. The regions differ in geography and in culture. In northern Louisiana, most residents are of British-American or African-American heritage, though there are smaller groups, such as Czechs, Germans, Italians, and Hungarians. Farming, ranching, and forestry have been traditional ways of life in the region. Natural gas and oil production have become important as well. Large cotton plantations once lined the valuable farmland along the riverbanks known as the "front lands." Away from the main riverbanks, in remote swamps and waterways, people struggled to earn a living in the region called the "back lands," where many still hunt, fish, and trap for income. Today, people who enjoy hunting, boating, and fishing think of the back lands as a special destination.

Set along the Red River, Shreveport is the largest city in northern Louisiana. Shreveport boomed in the 1830s after steamboat captain Henry Shreve cleared the Red River of a logjam that stretched more than 150 miles (240 km). Removing the Great Raft, as the logjam was known, opened up the river to boat traffic. During the Civil War, the city was the capital of Confederate Louisiana. Today, Shreveport is a busy, multicultural center for tourism, commerce, and manufacturing. It has become known as "Hollywood South" for the many movies filmed there.

Farther east is Grambling State University, a historically black college founded in 1901. South of Grambling is a former Native American trading post, Natchitoches, the oldest settlement in Louisiana. The city of Alexandria, near the geographic center of the state, also is the divide between cultural regions. The area is known as "the crossroads."

Southern Louisiana

Southern Louisiana has very deep French and Catholic roots. Yet the region also has influences from Spain, West Africa, the Caribbean, Mexico, Central America, and many parts of Europe and Asia, as well as from Native Americans. One group in particular has fashioned its own unique society. The region of the southwestern prairies and coastal bayous is known as Acadiana, the home of the Cajuns. Though many now work in offices, factories, oil fields, and other businesses, the Cajuns were traditionally fisher folk and farmers with a strong love of music, food, and family life.

African Americans, Germans, and people from Great Britain also migrated to the area. Many of the newcomers adopted the Cajun way of life, including speaking a distinct form of French. Today, Lake Charles is a thriving modern city located in Acadiana. The city of Lafayette, bursting with Cajun restaurants, music clubs, and museums, is one of the cultural centers of the region.

East of Acadiana are the state's largest cities, Baton Rouge and New Orleans. They are also two of the country's largest port cities, with giant docks that are always buzzing with activity, and huge storage facilities.

People in New Orleans take great pride in their city and its rich history. The city is known for its historic buildings with decorative ironwork and lush gardens. Nearly all houses have front porches or stoops. Before air conditioning, many people sat on their porches on hot days to catch any breeze that might blow in from the river.

A Taste of Louisiana

In northern Louisiana, food is prepared in much the same way it is in other Southern states. In southern Louisiana, there are two popular ways of cooking: Cajun and Creole. Gumbo is one very popular dish in Louisiana. It is also a symbol for the diversity of Louisianans. In the earliest days of the colony, the French prized a European recipe for a tasty seafood soup. In Louisiana, they learned to make do with local ingredients, such as shrimp and crawfish. Native Americans added native plants, herbs, and spices to the recipe. The Spanish added hot pepper sauce. African slaves who cooked for the Creole colonists added the vegetable okra. Cajuns contributed tomatoes, turtles, and alligators. Germans added smoked hams and sausages. During Lent (the period between the holy days of Ash Wednesday and Easter), Catholics followed a church rule limiting meat. So vegetables and herbs went into their gumbo recipes. Today, people throughout Louisiana have their own special recipes for gumbo.

Les Bon Temps [The Good Times]

From farmers' fields, city streets, and backwater bayous to church halls, riverboats, and clubs, the special music of Louisiana rings out. American music forms such as Western swing, blues, and gospel are heard throughout Louisiana.

When Cajuns first came to Louisiana, they brought Acadian fiddle music. After German farmers moved to Acadiana, they introduced the accordion to their Cajun neighbors. Since then, the accordion has been the soul of Cajun music. African Americans added washboard strumming and other rhythms to the Cajun sound to create the lively dance music called zydeco. New Orleans has long been famous for jazz. Early stars were Louis Armstrong and Jelly Roll Morton. Louisiana musicians Fats Domino and Jerry Lee Lewis were early rock 'n' roll stars. Today, New Orleans is one of the world's best cities for listening to jazz, blues, rock, gospel, Cajun, zydeco, hip-hop, and more.

Louisiana is rich in festivals. The French expression *Laissez les bon temps rouler*, which means "Let the good times roll," is often heard in Louisiana. There are many music festivals. The love of food is revealed in festivals devoted entirely to gumbo, jambalaya, oysters, pralines, meat pies, shrimp, catfish, crawfish, strawberries, and other foods. The ethnic heritage of the state is honored in festivals such as Czech Days, German Oktoberfest, Laotian New Year, Calling of the Tribes Powwow, and Isleños Festival.

Festivals celebrating religious holidays are also very important to Louisiana residents. In December, communities throughout the state celebrate the holiday season with a Festival of Lights. Mardi Gras, which in English means "Fat Tuesday," is a traditional Roman Catholic carnival that takes place just before Lent begins. Lent is a forty-day period between Ash Wednesday and Easter. According to the Christian faith, followers should deny themselves too much food, drink, and merriment during Lent. So Mardi Gras symbolizes the last chance until Easter for a lot of food, music, and fun.

There are Mardi Gras celebrations throughout the state, but one of the biggest in the world is in New Orleans. In that city, Mardi Gras is an official holiday. Citizens decorate the city in the official colors of gold, purple, and green. There are masked balls and parades for weeks leading up to Mardi Gras. People dressed in colorful feathers, beads, and glitter ride elaborate floats. On Mardi Gras, more than a million parade-goers line the streets and reach out to capture beads, festival coins, and other holiday trinkets thrown from the floats.

Louisiana's unique blend of ethnic and religious traditions has always helped it stand apart from other states. Citizens are proud of their culture.

10 KEY EVENTS ★ ★ ★

La Toussaint

Sugar Cane Festival

1. Festival International de Louisiane

The last week of April turns downtown Lafayette into a giant stage. Performers from such faraway places as Senegal, Brazil, Congo, and Quebec join popular Louisiana Cajun and zydeco musicians for a five-day celebration of music, food, art, and dance.

2. Frog Fest

The town of Rayne polishes the frog murals on its buildings and celebrates the common Louisiana swamp dweller. Festivities include a Frog Festival Queen's ball and the International Frog Racing and Jumping Contest.

3. La Toussaint

November 1, the day after Halloween, is All Saints' Day, a Catholic holiday that honors Christian saints. Louisianans call it La Toussaint. Every year, people across the state continue a tradition started by colonists—cleaning tombs and leaving flowers at graveyards.

4. Louisiana Sugar Cane Festival

Every September in Iberia Parish, Louisianans celebrate their Cajun heritage with parades, fireworks, a Cajun dance party, the crowning of Queen Sugar, and other sweet festivities.

5. Mudbug Madness

On Memorial Day weekend, Shreveport celebrates one of Louisiana's favorite activities—the crawfish boil. More than 60,000 pounds (27,200 kg) of crawfish are cooked while thousands of people pour into town to enter crawfish-eating contests, watch jugglers, and listen to music.

6. New Orleans Jazz and Heritage Festival

In spring, people from around the world visit New Orleans to hear some of the top acts in jazz and other styles of music. They also come to admire traditional and contemporary crafts, including decorative gourds and paintings, and to enjoy African, Cajun, Creole, Latino, and Native American food and culture.

7. Soul Fest

Held every March at the Audubon Zoo, Soul Fest celebrates African-American culture in Louisiana. More than 20,000 people gather to eat food, dance to music, and buy crafts. There are activities for kids and free health screenings as well.

8. State Fair of Louisiana

Shreveport hosts the state fair every year in the fall. It offers visitors food, rides, livestock and other animals, concerts, and various competitions. There is also a rodeo and circus.

9. Sugar Bowl

Each January, the Louisiana Superdome hosts one of college football's oldest bowl games. Two of the top teams in the country have met in the Sugar Bowl every year since 1934.

10. Swamp Fest at the Audubon Zoo

Thousands visit the Audubon Zoo in New Orleans in the fall to feed animals in the swamp exhibit, taste fried alligator and catfish po'boy sandwiches, and listen to Cajun and zydeco music.

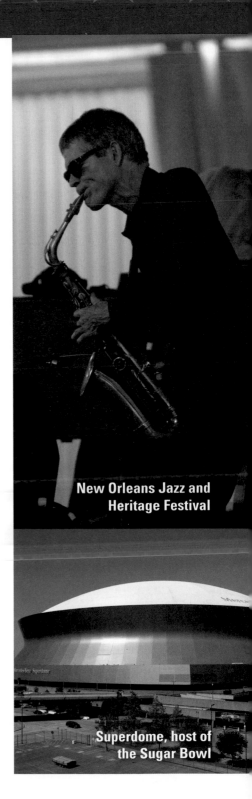

New Orleans Jazz and Heritage Festival

Superdome, host of the Sugar Bowl

At 450 feet (137 m) high and with 34 floors, the Louisiana State Capitol is the tallest state capitol building in the United States.

How the Government Works

There are three levels of government in Louisiana: city or town, parish, and state. In individual cities and towns, people elect mayors or **council** members to run the local government. Local government units made up of various towns and cities are called parishes in Louisiana. Most other states call these units counties. Louisiana's original Catholic parishes started under Spanish and French rule. In 1807, these boundaries were used to help mark regional governments. Voters in 41 of the state's 64 parishes elect a group called a police jury to manage their government. A few parishes have a commission and elect commissioners to run the government.

Branches of Government

Executive

The governor is the head of the executive branch. The people of Louisiana choose a governor every four years. He or she can serve only two terms in a row. The governor appoints cabinet members and signs bills into law.

Other executive branch offices include the lieutenant governor, attorney general, treasurer, and superintendent of education.

Louisiana Governor Bobby Jindal prepares to sign a bill into law.

Legislative

The legislative branch is made up of the state senate, with 39 members, and the state house of representatives, with 105 members. State legislators are elected for four-year terms and cannot be elected more than twice in a row. They meet each year for up to 60 working days. When not working at the Capitol in Baton Rouge, legislators meet with people in the

In Their Own Words

"Here's what I've found in Louisiana: The voters want to know what you believe, what you stand for, and what you plan to do, not what shade your skin is."
—Governor Bobby Jindal

area they represent. Often they hold other jobs, too, working as farmers, business owners, pharmacists, and lawyers.

Judicial

The judicial branch is a system of courts made up of the state supreme court, courts of appeal, and district courts. Most trials are decided by district courts. These courts hear criminal cases and settle

arguments over laws. The next level is the court of appeals. If someone does not believe he or she received a fair ruling in the district courts, court of appeals judges will hear the reasons and rule on whether to uphold or overturn the district court decision. Some cases are appealed from a court of appeals to the state supreme court for final ruling. The supreme court has a chief justice and six associate justices who are each elected from a separate district. Judges in the appeals and supreme courts serve ten-year terms.

At the level of state government, voters elect senators and representatives to the state **legislature**, judges, a governor, and other executive office holders. Like citizens in all other states, Louisianans also elect people to represent them in the U.S. Congress in Washington, D.C. As of 2014, Louisiana had six representatives in the U.S. House of Representatives. Voters elect one representative for their district every two years. Voters statewide elect two U.S. senators, who serve six-year terms.

How a Bill Becomes a Law

State senators and representatives, who together are called legislators, create and pass laws. A law can be started in either the state house of representatives or the state senate. To begin, a legislator proposes an idea for a law. Sometimes these ideas come from the state residents whom the legislator represents. The idea is spelled out in a document called a bill. The legislator who proposes it becomes the bill's sponsor. For example, in 2009, Louisiana Representative Nickie Monica wanted to encourage safety in motor vehicles. He proposed a bill that would fine people for not wearing seatbelts. "We know it's going to save lives," he said.

A clerk drafted Representative Monica's bill and assigned the bill a number (HB 499). Next the bill was read aloud in the house. Then the bill was assigned to a committee to discuss it. During committee meetings, members review bills and listen to people

New Orleans residents wait in line to vote in the November 2012 election.

who have come to talk about why they are in favor of or oppose a certain bill. After the meetings, the committee decides whether to approve the bill. If the committee approves the bill, it is then read out loud again. A bill must be read in each chamber on at least three separate occasions. At this time, all the representatives can debate the bill and suggest changes. Each time a bill is changed, or amended, the representatives vote.

Once the bill passed the house, it moved to the senate. There, it was reviewed by another committee. Once approved by the committee, the bill was amended and voted on. If the senate passes a bill but makes amendments, the bill must be returned to the house for review before being presented to the governor. If the house approves the changes, it delivers the bill to the governor for signature. If the governor signs the bill, it becomes law. Governor Bobby Jindal signed Representative Monica's bill, which became a law known as Act 166 of 2009.

However, the governor may veto, or refuse to sign, a bill. A vetoed bill is sent back to the legislature. There, lawmakers decide whether to let the bill fail or to override the governor's veto and pass the law. To override a veto, both houses must vote in favor of the bill by a two-thirds majority.

In July 2013, lawmakers and advocates attempted to override a veto session by Governor Jindal because they were unhappy with his decision to veto the expansion of programs for the disabled. A majority of both the House of Representatives and the Senate was needed to trigger the override session, however when voting took place, a majority was not reached.

Louisianans speak out to the government. Here, Louisiana protesters hold signs in an attempt to urge the U.S. Justice Department to hold oil company BP responsible in court for the oil spill in 2010.

POLITICAL FIGURES
FROM LOUISIANA

Lindy Boggs:
Member of U.S. Congress, 1973-1991

Marie Corinne Morrison Claiborne (Lindy) Boggs was born near New Roads, Louisiana in 1916. Boggs went to college and became a teacher. When her husband Hale died in a plane crash in 1972, Boggs ran for his seat in the U.S. House of Representatives. She won, becoming the first woman to represent Louisiana in Congress.

Bobby Jindal:
Governor of Louisiana, 2008-

Bobby Jindal was born in Baton Rouge in 1971. He studied biology and public policy in college. In 2004, Jindal was elected to the U.S. House of Representatives. He then became the first Indian-American governor in U.S. history when he was sworn in as governor of Louisiana in January 2008. He was re-elected in 2011.

Ray Nagin:
Mayor of New Orleans, 2002-2010

Born and raised in New Orleans, Ray Nagin worked in various businesses after graduating from college. He ran for mayor of New Orleans, and was elected in 2002. After Hurricane Katrina devastated New Orleans in 2005, Nagin criticized the government's emergency response. Nagin served another term as mayor from 2006 to 2010.

LOUISIANA
YOU CAN MAKE A DIFFERENCE

★ Contacting Lawmakers

Citizens can share their thoughts on an issue with any of Louisiana's state legislators.

Go to: **legis.state.la.us**

Scroll down the page and look under "Your Louisiana Legislators." The linked page will help citizens find the legislators who represent the area in which they live.

★ Speaking Up

Louisianans have always known the power of the people. Louisiana's citizens and lawmakers know that everyone's voices are important, and citizens throughout the state's long history have fought for fair and equal rights.

For example, in 1960, a Louisiana first grader and her family spoke out against racial inequality in schools. Ruby Bridges was a young African-American girl who had moved to New Orleans with her family. The federal government in Washington, D.C., had ordered New Orleans to desegregate its schools. Black students could no longer be kept out of white schools. This angered many white people in the city. On November 14, 1960, six-year-old Ruby Bridges walked beside four federal marshals through an angry crowd of white protesters to enter an all-white elementary school. When Ruby returned to school the next day, she walked into an empty classroom. All the white families had taken their children out of school. Each day after that, Ruby's teacher taught her only student. And each day, Ruby walked past protesters yelling and throwing things at her on the way to school. A year later, the school was fully integrated. Ruby was no longer the only black student in the building, and white and black students attended the school together.

Few children are expected to act as bravely as Ruby Bridges, but all students should speak up for what they believe in. Desegregation occurred because people fought for what they believed was right. They voiced their opinions and influenced legislators to create laws for equality. This still holds true today. Each year, Louisiana state legislators visit hundreds of public schools and tell the students, "Your ideas count!"

In 2011, Louisiana produced 511,000 bales of cotton.

Making a Living

Louisianans have lived through difficult cycles of economic gain and loss. For example, many people lost their livelihood as a result of Hurricane Katrina in 2005. But from 2005 to 2008, the average Louisianan's income increased by nearly half. Most of the increase was the result of financial aid from the U.S. government. State leaders also took steps to improve conditions for citizens. Louisiana fared better than most states when economic troubles caused millions of people nationwide to lose their jobs in 2008 and 2009. There are many reasons why a greater percentage of people born in Louisiana choose to stay in their home state than natives of any other state.

Agriculture

Louisiana is blessed with rich soil and a climate that is ideal for growing a variety of crops. The major crops are cotton, sugar, rice, corn, and soybeans. There are more than 8 million acres (3.2 million hectares) of farmland in the state. Louisiana's crops are sold throughout the country.

Rice is an important crop to Louisiana farmers. African slaves first brought rice seed to the Louisiana prairies as early as 1718. Rice grew well in the wet soil, but it did not become popular until after the Civil War. In the 1800s, Cajun and German rice farmers used

A farmer in south Louisiana stands on part of his rice harvest.

floodwaters from the Mississippi River to grow rice. Residents later developed irrigation channels to provide the water for the crop. In the 1950s, rice farmers added crawfish to their flooded fields. After the farmers harvested the rice, the crawfish would eat algae and rotting plant matter. The crawfish could later be harvested for food, providing a second crop. In addition to providing crops, the crawfish–rice fields have become important wetlands for wildlife.

More than a quarter of Louisiana is covered by farms. A third of that land is used for pasture and livestock. Grass grows year-round in the warm, wet climate, so cattle have plenty of fresh grazing land. Farmers also raise hogs and goats. But despite the variety of crops and livestock, fewer people have jobs in farming each year. Large corporations and successful landowners now operate about half of the state's farmland. These large farms earn greater profits and can afford expensive farm machinery. The machines are extremely efficient and do much of the work once done by farm laborers.

Fishing

More than a billion pounds of fish and shellfish are harvested in the state each year. Louisiana's commercial fishers catch about 25 percent of all seafood in the United States. The state produces more shrimp and oysters than any other state. Other prized seafood includes crab, red snapper, and yellowfin tuna. Freshwater fishers catch crawfish and catfish. But these creatures are also raised in fish farms.

A worker unloads a haul from a shrimp boat in the small coastal town of Empire, Louisiana.

★ 10 KEY INDUSTRIES ★

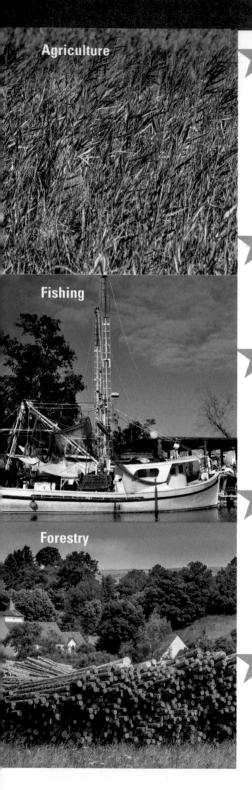

Agriculture

Fishing

Forestry

1. Agriculture

Louisiana is a large producer of pecans, sweet potatoes, rice, and sugarcane. Sugarcane has been grown in Louisiana since the 1700s. Today, sugarcane fields in Louisiana yield 30 to 50 tons (27-45 metric tons) of sugarcane per acre. From each ton, 175 to 225 pounds (79 to 102 kg) of sugar is produced.

2. Chemicals

Louisiana produces 25 percent of the nation's petrochemicals, which are chemicals made from petroleum. The total value of chemical shipments is more than $14 billion a year.

3. Fishing

Commercial fishing in Louisiana produces around 25 percent of America's seafood, particularly shrimp. Brown shrimp are most abundant in late spring and early summer. White shrimp are harvested in late summer and early fall.

4. Tabasco Sauce

After the Civil War, Edmund McIlhenny returned to his plantation on Avery Island to find everything destroyed, except his special Mexican hot peppers. He used the peppers to create Tabasco hot sauce. Today, the McIlhenny family's company sells millions of bottles of the spicy sauce each year.

5. Forestry

Louisiana has more than 13.9 million acres of forests. Around 3.6 million cords of wood are cut each year to make paper, plywood, furniture, and other products.

LOUISIANA

 6. Healthcare

In the last 40 years, the number of people employed in healthcare in Louisiana has grown 400 percent.

 7. Manufacturing

Some of the goods Louisiana produces are telephone systems, electrical equipment, and automotive batteries. Special manufacturing plants in Louisiana produce **ammonia** from the **hydrogen** in natural gas. Much of the ammonia is used in the fertilizers that help plants grow. The Baton Rouge area makes about a quarter of America's ammonia.

 8. Oil

Supertankers need very deep water to dock and a lot of room to move around. Only one port in the country has waters deep enough to unload oil from these giant tankers—the Louisiana Offshore Oil Port. The "superport" was completed in 1981. The oil is pumped from the tankers and sent to shore by underwater pipelines.

 9. Ports

Louisiana has the nation's farthest inland port, in Baton Rouge. The "superport" is the country's only port that can handle large tankers. More than 25 percent of the nation's waterborne exports are shipped through Louisiana's five ports.

 10. Tourism

Travelers once spent more than $10 billion a year in the state. The effects of Hurricane Katrina lowered tourism income, but only so many visitors can stay away. New Orleans, historic plantations, and the music of Acadiana are just some of the attractions that still draw millions of visitors every year.

Healthcare

Oil

Ports

Recipe for King Cake

King cake is a traditional, colorful cake eaten at home or at parties in Louisiana during Mardi Gras. King cake is round, and it is usually decorated with gold, purple, and green icing or sprinkles. Follow this easy recipe with the help of an adult and enjoy this delicious treat!

What You Need

1 can of Pillsbury breadsticks
1 can of cream cheese frosting
¼ cup (177 milliliters) heavy cream
Green, purple, and yellow sprinkles

What to Do

- Preheat oven to 400°F (200C°).
- Line a baking sheet with parchment paper.
- Open bread sticks. Press together the ends of two of the sticks to make one long stick. Repeat with the remaining bread sticks until you have six long sticks.
- Taking three at a time, loosely braid the sticks together. Repeat with remaining dough.
- Pinch the braids together end to end.
- Leaving a 3-inch (7 cm) hole in the middle, loosely coil braids around one another on the baking sheet. Press ends together.
- Bake for 18 to 20 minutes or until golden brown.
- Remove from oven and cool completely.
- In a medium pot, combine the cream cheese frosting and heavy cream. Have an adult help you with this step.
- Heat over low heat until warm and smooth, stirring constantly.
- Pour glaze over cake and sprinkle with sprinkles.

Louisiana has tens of thousands of jobs in the fishing industry. Besides fishing, people work at selling, shipping, processing, and packaging fish. Thousands of others build and maintain boats, gear, and supplies for the fishing industry.

Forestry and Wood Products

More than half of Louisiana is covered by forests. Pine, oak, sweetgum, cypress, and other trees are harvested. More than 25,000 people have jobs cutting, transporting, or processing timber. Wood in Louisiana is used to make paper, boxes, shopping bags, furniture, and construction materials, as well as baseball bats, musical instruments, and boats. Each year, the forest and forest products industries add about $3 billion to the economy of the state.

Natural Gas, Oil, Mining, and Manufacturing

In the 1870s, companies drilled wells in search of water to make ice. One evening, a night watchman at an ice factory in Shreveport felt wind coming from a well that was being drilled. When he lit a match to investigate, he caused an explosion. Natural gas, not water, had been flowing through the pipe. Gas from the well was soon piped to the factory to provide energy for lighting. This was the beginning of Louisiana's oil and natural gas industry.

The first successful oil well in Louisiana was drilled in 1901 near the town of Jennings, a farming community halfway between Lafayette and Lake Charles. Since that time, rice farmers and swamp fishers along the coast have lived and worked side by side with oil field workers. After World War II, major oil fields were discovered in the Gulf of Mexico. In 1947, the first drilling platforms were built offshore out of sight of land. Today, Louisiana is the nation's fourth-largest producer of oil.

But the state does not just drill the oil. Louisiana's ports also bring in a fifth of the foreign oil used by Americans. The state is a very important storage center for oil and natural gas. Massive salt caves have been filled with oil for emergencies. Dozens of pipelines deliver oil and natural gas from Louisiana to states as far away as Wisconsin.

Louisiana's mines provide important minerals such as sulfur and salt. Louisiana has huge underground rock salt formations. Some are 50,000 feet (15,240 m) deep and stretch for a mile across. In 1862, the nation's first rock salt mine was dug on Avery Island. Salt is commonly used for cooking, but it also has uses in paper-making, soap-making, fabric-dyeing, and other areas of manufacturing. Around the country, millions of pounds of rock salt are used each winter to de-ice roads and make them safe for driving.

The Louisiana Gulf Coast is key to the nation's petrochemical industry. Petrochemical refineries are factories that turn crude oil and natural gas liquids into plastics, fertilizers, synthetic (human-made) rubber, and other products.

People in the state also make well-drilling platforms, ships of all sizes, small trucks, telephones, glass, marine radar, clothing, and hundreds of other products.

Transportation

Steamboats began traveling the Mississippi River in 1811, carrying cargo to and from New Orleans. Louisiana has the nation's second-largest number of navigable waterways. Today, there are more than 30 ports in the state. The Port of South Louisiana is the nation's largest by tonnage carried. It spans the area between New Orleans and Baton Rouge. Nearby, the Port of New Orleans handles more dry bulk cargo than any other port in the country. Dry bulk products such as corn from the Midwest can be poured into large holds in a ship and sucked out at their destination. Deepwater docks at these ports have nearby storage facilities for foods such as tropical fruits and coffee beans. Dock areas also have grain silos, oil tanks, and steel yards and lumberyards. Using natural rivers and lakes and human-made channels, Louisiana has created an intracoastal waterway. It allows ocean freighters to travel the entire coastline, safe from storms in the Gulf of Mexico. About one in seven jobs in the state depends on its waterways. The ports at Baton Rouge and Lake Charles are also huge contributors to the state's economy.

Destination: New Orleans

A large portion of tourism in Louisiana is centered in New Orleans. The "Big Easy" is full of world-famous theaters, museums, restaurants, and music clubs. Football fans flock to the Superdome to cheer for the New Orleans Saints. Visitors spend more than $5 billion in the city each year. One-fourth of that is spent during the famous Mardi Gras celebration.

Many people visit Louisiana to see its amazing architecture. Each year, people come to admire buildings designed in European and Caribbean styles in New Orleans. Throughout the state, visitors can see historic buildings, traditional plantations, and other sites that serve as reminders of the state's past.

Ecotourism

A newer addition to the tourism industry is ecotourism. Ecotourism is travel based on viewing nature and wildlife, such as bird-watching or taking a swamp tour. But Louisiana's swamps and coastal wetlands have been seriously suffering. Each year, about 24 square miles (62 sq km) of coastal wetlands are washed away. That equals the loss of land area the size of a football field every forty-five minutes. In the past, the Mississippi River naturally changed directions, bringing soil from lands farther upriver to create "new land" in the delta. But thousands of human-made levees, dams, and channels along the Mississippi and the rivers that feed into it have directed the water away from its natural course. New wetlands are not being naturally created to make up for the land lost each year. The wetlands protect wildlife, but they also protect the coastline from the Gulf of Mexico's violent storms.

The enormous burden of maintaining and protecting the wetlands is more than the state can handle alone. Louisiana's leaders want the federal government to provide more help. They want states farther north along the Mississippi to contribute, too. Louisiana's seafood harvest is shipped around the nation. Most of the continent's migratory birds stop over in the Pelican State. The problems of coastal Louisiana are the problems of the entire United States. Ecotours into these unique regions teach visitors what every resident already knows: Louisiana is a special place.

Local kids catch beads from a float during Mardi Gras.

LOUISIANA

N
W E
S

NEW ORLEANS AREA

Kenner · Metairie · New Orleans
River Ridge · Jefferson · Chalmette
Westwego · Gretna
Marrero · Harvey

Caddo Lake
Black Bayou
Shreveport
Minden
D'Arbonne National Wildlife Refuge
Upper Ouachita National Wildlife Refuge
Handy Brake National Wildlife Refuge
Bastrop
Bayou D'Arbonne Lake
Bayou Lafourche
Monroe
Ruston
Bayou Macon
Tallulah
DRISKILL MOUNTAIN
Black Lake Bayou
Toledo Bend Reservoir
Natchitoches
Bayou Pierre
Black Lake
Red River
Kisatchie National Forest
Catahoula National Wildlife Refuge
Catahoula Lake
Tensas River National Wildlife Refuge
Bayou Cocodrie National Wildlife Refuge
Mississippi River
Alexandria
Alexander State Forest
Fort Polk
Lake Ophelia National Wildlife Refuge
Bayou Amacoco
Sabine River
Bayou Nezpique
Bayou Teche
Calcasieu River
Opelousas
Eunice
New Roads
TUNICA HILLS
Bogalusa
Hammond
Baton Rouge
Lake Pontchartrain
Slidell
Lake Borgne
Moss Bluff
Sulphur
Lake Charles
Jennings
Crowley
Lafayette
Abbeville
New Iberia
Chitimacha Indian Reservation
La Place
New Orleans
Chandeleur Sound
Breton National Wildlife Refuge
Sabine National Wildlife Refuge
Lacassine National Wildlife Refuge
Calcasieu Lake
Cameron Prairie National Wildlife Refuge
Sabine Lake
INTRACOASTAL WATERWAY
Grand Lake
White Lake
Marsh Island
Weeks Bay
Vermilion Bay
Raceland
Jean Lafitte National Historic Park
Breton Sound
Rockefeller State Wildlife Refuge
Marsh Island State Wildlife Refuge
Shell Keys National Wildlife Refuge
Morgan City
Atchafalaya River
Houma
Barataria Bay
Delta National Wildlife Refuge
East Cote Blanche Bay
Caillou Bay
Timbalier Bay
Terrebonne Bay
MISSISSIPPI RIVER DELTA
Pilottown
GULF OF MEXICO
GULF OF MEXICO

miles
0   30

Interstate Highway
U.S. Highway
State Highway
State Capital
City or Town
Wildlife Refuge
Highest Point in the State
Indian Reservation
National Forest
State Forest
National Historic Park

LOUISIANA
MAP SKILLS

1. What is Louisiana's highest point?

2. What three bodies of water sit along Louisiana's western border?

3. Which national wildlife refuge is located outside of Pilottown?

4. What state highway runs across the northern part of the state?

5. Alexander State Forest is located near what city?

6. What is the name of the Indian reservation northwest of Morgan City?

7. What U.S. highway would you take to go from Shreveport to Moss Bluff?

8. Interstate 12 connects what two cities?

9. What waterway runs along the southern coast of Louisiana to the Gulf of Mexico?

10. Bayou Cocodrie National Wildlife Refuge is located near what river?

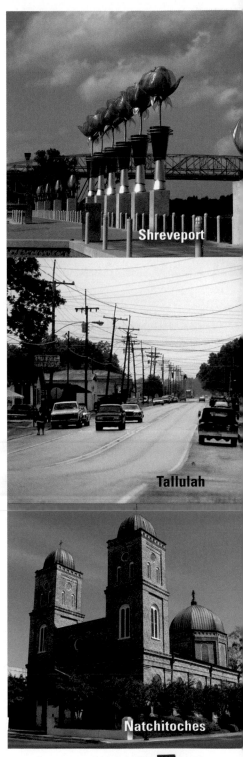

Shreveport

Tallulah

Natchitoches

10. Mississippi River
9. Intracoastal Waterway
8. Baton Rouge and Slidell
7. 171
6. Chitimacha Indian Reservation
5. Alexandria
4. 2
3. Delta National Wildlife Refuge
2. Caddo Lake, Toledo Bend Reservoir, and Sabine Lake
1. Driskill Mountain

State Seal, Flag, and Song

The official state seal looks a lot like the flag. It was adopted in 1902. Inside the circle is a pelican in a nest with three of her young. The mother pelican is picking at her chest to feed her young rather than letting them starve. The original description of the seal and flag described the mother pelican as having three drops of blood on her chest, but over time, the drops were left out. In 2010, the seal was officially changed and includes the drops of blood again.

The people of Louisiana kept true to its nickname, the Pelican State, by adopting this flag in 1912. A pelican feeds its young, centered on a solid blue background. Underneath the pelicans' nest is a white ribbon that bears the state motto: "Union, Justice and Confidence." Previous versions of the flag (and seal) had as many as 12 baby pelicans on it, however pelicans rarely have more than three.

To see the lyrics of the Louisiana State Song, "You Are My Sunshine," go to
www.statesymbolsusa.org/Louisiana/LAstatesongsunshine.html

Glossary

ammonia A colorless gas or liquid that has a strong smell and taste and that is used especially in cleaning products.

bankrupt An individual or group whose property by court order is turned over to be managed for the benefit of the creditors.

collide To come together with solid or direct impact.

council A group of people who are chosen to make rules, laws, or decisions about something.

debris The pieces that are left after something has been destroyed.

endangered In danger of no longer existing.

fertilizers Substances that are added to soil to help the growth of plants.

hydrogen A chemical element that has no color or smell and is the simplest, lightest, and most common element.

immigrants People who come to a country to live there.

indigo A blue dye obtained from plants.

legislature A group of people with the power to make or change laws.

naturalist A person who studies plants and animals as they live in nature.

nomadic Roaming about from place to place aimlessly, frequently, or without a fixed pattern of movement.

petroleum A kind of oil that comes from below the ground and is the source of gasoline and other products.

pirates People who attack and steal from ships at sea.

refugees People who have been forced to leave a country because of war or for religious or political reasons.

More About Louisiana

BOOKS

Benoit, Peter. *Hurricane Katrina*. New York, NY. Scholastic, 2011.

Brasseaux, Carl A. *Acadiana: Louisiana's Historic Cajun Country*. Baton Rouge, LA: Louisiana State University Press, 2011.

Coleman, Miriam. *Louisiana: The Pelican State*. New York, NY: PowerKids Press, 2011.

Lynette, Rachel. *The Louisiana Purchase*. New York, NY: PowerKids Press, 2013.

McGee, Randel. *Paper Crafts for Mardi Gras*. Berkeley Heights, NJ: Enslow Elementary, 2011.

WEBSITES

Louisiana Department of Culture, Recreation, and Tourism:

www.crt.state.la.us

Louisiana House of Representatives Kids' Page:

house.legis.state.la.us/pubinfo/Kids.htm

The Official State of Louisiana Kids' Page:

www.louisiana.gov/Explore/Kids_Page

ABOUT THE AUTHORS

Ruth Bjorklund lives on Bainbridge Island, across Puget Sound from Seattle, Washington, with her husband, two children, and many pets. Ruth has written several nonfiction books for students on a variety of topics. She has visited every state in the country, and Louisiana is definitely a favorite.

Andy Steinitz has written and edited educational and reference materials for The World Almanac, Borders Books, and The New York Times. He thanks his many Cajun friends who fed him gumbo and crawfish for inspiration. Steinitz currently works at Pratt Institute. He lives in Brooklyn, N.Y.

Index

Page numbers in **boldface** are illustrations.

Index